SCOM TOOLS

SOURCE CODE

Using VB.Net to create them

Richard Thomas Edwards

Building a future from building a strong past

I just didn't know WMI was going to pave the way

F THERE IS ONE THING I KNOW FOR SURE, I wouldn't be writing this e-book and --a few others on SCOM --had I not invested my time and effort learning WMI and how to use scripting tools such as Jscript, Perlscript, PowerShell and VBScript. Does that surprise you with all the WbemScripting titles for all my e-books?

Well, I pretty much stayed clear of WMI here. Using it in the Event Log program.

With that said, this book is about creating some basic tools that will help you perform some of the tasks needed to work with SCOM and System Center Service Manager also known as SCSM or Service Manager. Service Manager was built on top of SCOM and uses Management Packs and Bundled Management Packs in the same way as SCOM does.

I have an entire e-book coming soon that will cover building Management Packs dynamically and perform some cool things. Right now, I'm covering the following:

- Sealing and unsealing Management Packs
- Bundling and unbundling Management Pack Bundles
- Building a customized Event Log Viewer and Event Log writer

I have also included a group of stylesheets you can add to the html piece of the Event Log Viewer that will make the output look different and more robust.

Before we get started: A couple of tricks and tips

am not one for bragging but this is the type of book I was looking for. book rocks! You are about to go on a journey that for the past 10 years has helped me maintain an annual salary of $100,000. You ready?

Let's begin with a few tips that you may not know about SCOM.

One, inside the Microsoft.EnterpriseManagement.Core.dll, starting at line 1294, you will find the entire developer reference. Xsd for developing a Management Pack.

Two, you don't have to have System Center Configuration Manager -- SCOM for short-- installed to start writing programs you will be using quite regularly. Simply copy the Microsoft.EnterpriseManagement.Core.dll inside your project debug folder and create a reference to it through visual studio.

Three, You can create, read and revise Management Packs by just using the Microsoft.EnterpriseManagement.Core.dll without having to connect to SCOM. Which was one of the reasons why Microsoft came up with the Management Pack Authoring Console.

Sealing and unsealing a Management Packs

Just don't unseal third party Management Packs without permission

W HEN SCOM 2007 came out, unsealing a Management Pack was the way you learned how to read the XML and understand what was under the hood. After all, Microsoft basically, the only company building SCOM Management Packs and since we were writing Management Packs for the launch of Windows 2008, it was the only way someone like myself could learn how to create and script one.

Of course, today, there are a lot of 3rd party software vendors that produce Management Packs and some of them get mad and could sue you if you unseal their MP. Just had to say that to cover my butt.

UNSEALING A MANAGEMENT PACK

It takes three lines to Unseal a ManagementPack:

Dim mp as new ManagementPack(fullpath and filename)

Dim writer as new ManagementPackXmlWriter(Application.StartupPath)

```
Dim xmlfilename = writer.WriteManagementPack(mp)
```

SEALING A MANAGEMENTPACK

This takes a bit more work than just three lines:

```vbnet
Imports Microsoft.EnterpriseManagement.Configuration
Imports Microsoft.EnterpriseManagement.Configuration.IO
Public Class Form1

Private Sub Button2_Click(ByVal sender As System.Object, ByVal e
As System.EventArgs) Handles Button2.Click
OpenFileDialog1.Filter = "*.xml|*.xml"
OpenFileDialog1.FileName = ""
OpenFileDialog1.ShowDialog()
If (OpenFileDialog1.FileName <> "") Then

TextBox1.Text = OpenFileDialog1.FileName

End If
End Sub

Private Sub Button3_Click(ByVal sender As System.Object, ByVal e
As System.EventArgs) Handles Button3.Click
Dim dialog = New FolderBrowserDialog()
dialog.SelectedPath = Application.StartupPath
If DialogResult.OK = dialog.ShowDialog() Then
TextBox2.Text = dialog.SelectedPath
End If

End Sub

Private Sub Button4_Click(ByVal sender As System.Object, ByVal e
As System.EventArgs) Handles Button4.Click
Dim dialog = New FolderBrowserDialog()
dialog.SelectedPath = Application.StartupPath
If DialogResult.OK = dialog.ShowDialog() Then
TextBox3.Text = dialog.SelectedPath
End If
End Sub

Private Sub Button5_Click(ByVal sender As System.Object, ByVal e
As System.EventArgs) Handles Button5.Click
Dim dialog = New FolderBrowserDialog()
dialog.SelectedPath = Application.StartupPath
```

```vbnet
If DialogResult.OK = dialog.ShowDialog() Then
TextBox5.Text = dialog.SelectedPath
End If
End Sub

Private Sub Button1_Click(ByVal sender As System.Object, ByVal e
As System.EventArgs) Handles Button1.Click

If TextBox1.Text <> "" Then
If TextBox2.Text <> "" Then
If TextBox3.Text <> "" Then
If TextBox4.Text <> "" Then
If TextBox5.Text <> "" Then
Dim companyname As String = TextBox4.Text
Dim snkLocation As String = TextBox3.Text & "\WME.snk"
Dim libLocation As String = TextBox2.Text
Dim sealedMP As String = TextBox5.Text

Try
Dim mp As New ManagementPack(TextBox1.Text)
Dim mpWriterSettings As ManagementPackAssemblyWriterSettings =
New ManagementPackAssemblyWriterSettings(companyname,
snkLocation, False)
mpWriterSettings.OutputDirectory = sealedMP
Dim mpwriter As ManagementPackAssemblyWriter = New
ManagementPackAssemblyWriter(mpWriterSettings)
Dim iret As String = mpwriter.WriteManagementPack(mp)

MsgBox("The " + TextBox1.Text + " Management Pack is now
sealed.")
Catch ex As Exception
MsgBox(ex.Message)
End Try

End If
End If
End If
End If
End If
End Sub
End Class
```

And here's what the form that helps make this magic happen looks like:

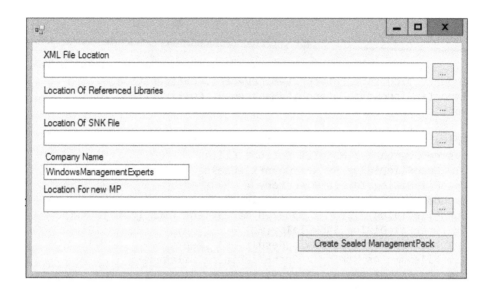

The code key code that makes this work is:

```
Dim mp As New ManagementPack(TextBox1.Text)
Dim mpWriterSettings As ManagementPackAssemblyWriterSettings =
New ManagementPackAssemblyWriterSettings(companyname,
snkLocation, False)

mpWriterSettings.OutputDirectory = sealedMP

Dim mpwriter As ManagementPackAssemblyWriter = New
ManagementPackAssemblyWriter(mpWriterSettings)

Dim iret As String = mpwriter.WriteManagementPack(mp)
```

So, if you have a snk file, a company name and the location where all the referenced and sealed mps are located, the code will seal your MP.

But this also leads to another question. This is a discover MP and you plan on referencing it in a Monitoring.mp you are working with. How do you get the ID?

Here's the code:

```
Imports Microsoft.EnterpriseManagement.Configuration
Imports Microsoft.EnterpriseManagement.Configuration.IO
Public Class Form1

Private Sub Button1_Click(sender As System.Object, e As
System.EventArgs) Handles Button1.Click
Dim OpenFileDialog As New OpenFileDialog
OpenFileDialog.InitialDirectory =
My.Computer.FileSystem.SpecialDirectories.MyDocuments
OpenFileDialog.Filter = "Sealed Management Pack (*.mp)| *.mp"
If (OpenFileDialog.ShowDialog(Me) =
System.Windows.Forms.DialogResult.OK) Then
Dim FileName As String = OpenFileDialog.FileName
Dim pos As Integer = InStrRev(FileName, "\")
TextBox1.Text = Mid(FileName, 1, pos - 1)
TextBox2.Text = Mid(FileName, pos + 2, Len(FileName))
Dim mp As New ManagementPack(FileName)
TextBox3.Text = mp.KeyToken
End If
End Sub

End Class
```

Here' the IDE view:

Path

I:

Filename

CDHHSProjectIntake.mp

Public Key Token:

805dfe111719803d

This one is pretty much cut and dry. Find the mp and then open it and display the Public Key Token.

Bundling and Unbundling
The life and times of a mpb file

BUNDLING

```vbnet
Imports Microsoft.EnterpriseManagement
Imports Microsoft.EnterpriseManagement.Common
Imports Microsoft.EnterpriseManagement.Configuration
Imports Microsoft.EnterpriseManagement.Configuration.IO
Imports Microsoft.EnterpriseManagement.Packaging
Imports System.Text
Imports System.IO
Public Class Form1

Dim mg As
Microsoft.EnterpriseManagement.EnterpriseManagementGroup
Dim bundle As ManagementPackBundle
Dim bundleWriter As ManagementPackBundleWriter
Dim mp As ManagementPack

Private Sub Button3_Click(sender As System.Object, e As
System.EventArgs) Handles Button3.Click

If TextBox3.Text = "" AndAlso TextBox4.Text = "" Then
MsgBox("Please supply the name of your Management pack bundle
before clicking here.")
Exit Sub
```

```vb
    End If

    If TextBox1.Text = "" AndAlso TextBox2.Text = "" Then
    MsgBox("Please supply the name of your Managementpack before
    clicking here.")
    Exit Sub
    End If

    Create_The_Bundle()
    Add_The_MP()
    Add_The_Resources()
    Bundle_And_Close_The_File()


    End Sub

    Private Sub Button1_Click(sender As System.Object, e As
    System.EventArgs) Handles Button1.Click

    Dim OpenFileDialog As New OpenFileDialog
    OpenFileDialog.InitialDirectory =
    My.Computer.FileSystem.SpecialDirectories.MyDocuments
    OpenFileDialog.Filter = "Sealed ManagementPack
    (*.mp)|*.mp|UnSealed ManagementPack (*.xml)|*.xml"
    If (OpenFileDialog.ShowDialog(Me) =
    System.Windows.Forms.DialogResult.OK) Then
    Dim FileName As String = OpenFileDialog.FileName
    Dim pos As Integer = InStrRev(FileName, "\")
    TextBox1.Text = Mid(FileName, 1, pos - 1)
    TextBox2.Text = Mid(FileName, pos + 1, Len(FileName))
    End If

    End Sub

    Private Sub Button2_Click(sender As System.Object, e As
    System.EventArgs) Handles Button2.Click

    Dim SaveFileDialog As New SaveFileDialog

    SaveFileDialog.InitialDirectory =
    My.Computer.FileSystem.SpecialDirectories.MyDocuments
    SaveFileDialog.Filter = "ManagementPackBundle (*.mpb)|*.mpb"

    If (SaveFileDialog.ShowDialog(Me) =
    System.Windows.Forms.DialogResult.OK) Then
```

```vbnet
Dim FileName As String = SaveFileDialog.FileName
Dim pos As Integer = InStrRev(FileName, "\")
TextBox3.Text = Mid(FileName, 1, pos - 1)
TextBox4.Text = Mid(FileName, pos + 1, Len(FileName))

End If

End Sub

Private Sub Button4_Click(sender As System.Object, e As
System.EventArgs) Handles Button4.Click

Dim FolderDialog As New FolderBrowserDialog
FolderDialog.ShowNewFolderButton = True
If (FolderDialog.ShowDialog() = DialogResult.OK) Then
Dim fso As Object = CreateObject("Scripting.FileSystemObject")
Dim fldr As Object = fso.GetFolder(FolderDialog.SelectedPath)
ListView1.Items.Clear()
For Each F As Object In fldr.Files
Dim pos As Integer = InStrRev(F.Path, "\")
Dim fl As String = Mid(F.Path, 1, pos - 1)
Dim li As ListViewItem = ListView1.Items.Add(fl)
li.SubItems.Add(F.Name)
Next

End If

End Sub
Public Sub Create_The_Bundle()

bundleWriter =
ManagementPackBundleFactory.CreateBundleWriter(TextBox3.Text)
bundle = ManagementPackBundleFactory.CreateBundle()

End Sub

Public Sub Add_The_MP()
mp = New ManagementPack(TextBox1.Text & "\" & TextBox2.Text)
bundle.ManagementPacks.Add(mp)
End Sub

Public Sub Add_The_Resources()

Dim fso As Object = CreateObject("Scripting.FileSystemObject")
```

```vbnet
Dim resources As System.Collections.Generic.IDictionary(Of
String, System.IO.FileStream) = New Dictionary(Of String,
System.IO.FileStream)

For x As Integer = 0 To ListView1.Items.Count - 1

Dim fpath As String = ListView1.Items(x).Text & "\" &
ListView1.Items(x).SubItems(1).Text

Dim fs As System.IO.FileStream = New System.IO.FileStream(fpath,
System.IO.FileMode.Open)
Dim fn As String = ListView1.Items(x).SubItems(1).Text
Dim pos As Integer = InStrRev(fn, ".")
If pos Then
fn = Mid(fn, 1, pos - 1)
End If

Try
bundle.AddResourceStream(mp, fn, fs,
ManagementPackBundleStreamSignature.Empty)

Catch ex As Exception

Err.Clear()

End Try


Next

End Sub

Public Sub Bundle_And_Close_The_File()

Dim fn As String = TextBox4.Text
Dim pos As Integer = InStrRev(fn, ".")
If pos Then
fn = Mid(fn, 1, pos - 1)
End If

Try

bundleWriter.Write(bundle, fn)
MsgBox(TextBox3.Text & "\" & TextBox4.Text & " has been
successfully been bundled.")
```

```
Catch ex As Exception

MsgBox(TextBox3.Text & "\" & TextBox4.Text & " Failed To Bundle
with " & ex.Message)

End Try


End Sub
```

The IDE Form looks like this:

UNBUNDLING

Here's the code for unbundling:

```
Imports Microsoft.EnterpriseManagement
Imports Microsoft.EnterpriseManagement.Common
Imports Microsoft.EnterpriseManagement.Configuration
```

```vb
Imports Microsoft.EnterpriseManagement.Configuration.IO
Imports Microsoft.EnterpriseManagement.Packaging
Imports System.Text
Imports System.IO
Public Class Form1

Private Sub Button3_Click(sender As System.Object, e As
System.EventArgs) Handles Button3.Click

Dim mystore As New ManagementPackFileStore
mystore.AddDirectory(Application.StartupPath)
Dim mpb As
Microsoft.EnterpriseManagement.Packaging.ManagementPackBundle
Dim mpbReader As
Microsoft.EnterpriseManagement.Packaging.ManagementPackBundleRead
er =
Microsoft.EnterpriseManagement.Packaging.ManagementPackBundleFact
ory.CreateBundleReader()
mpb = mpbReader.Read(TextBox1.Text & "\" & TextBox2.Text,
mystore)
Dim mpWriter As New
Microsoft.EnterpriseManagement.Configuration.IO.ManagementPackXml
Writer(Application.StartupPath)
For Each mp As ManagementPack In mpb.ManagementPacks()
mpWriter.WriteManagementPack(mp)
Dim fso As Object = CreateObject("Scripting.FileSystemObject")
If fso.FolderExists(Application.StartupPath & "\" &
Replace(mp.Name, ".", "_")) = False Then
fso.CreateFolder(Application.StartupPath & "\" & Replace(mp.Name,
".", "_"))
End If
Dim myfiles As System.Collections.Generic.IDictionary(Of String,
System.IO.Stream) = mpb.GetStreams(mp)

For Each key In myfiles.Keys

Dim mpElement As ManagementPackElement =
mp.FindManagementPackElementByName(key)
Dim fileName As String = mpElement.Name
Dim fdir As String = ""
'Dim actualBuffer As Byte()


''write to file
```

```vb
        Dim outputPath As String = Application.StartupPath & "\" &
        Replace(mp.Name, ".", "_") & "\" & key
        Dim incStream As MemoryStream = myfiles(key)
        Dim outputBytes(incStream.Length) As Byte

        incStream.Position = 0
        incStream.Read(outputBytes, 0, incStream.Length)


        Dim file As New System.IO.FileStream(outputPath,
        System.IO.FileMode.Create, System.IO.FileAccess.Write)
        file.Write(outputBytes, 0, outputBytes.Length)
        file.Close()

    Next

    Next

    MsgBox(TextBox1.Text & "\" & TextBox2.Text & " has been
    successfully been unbundled.")

    End Sub

    Private Sub Button1_Click(sender As System.Object, e As
    System.EventArgs) Handles Button1.Click

    Dim OpenFileDialog As New OpenFileDialog
    OpenFileDialog.InitialDirectory =
    My.Computer.FileSystem.SpecialDirectories.MyDocuments
    OpenFileDialog.Filter = "Text Files (*.mpb)|*.mpb"
    If (OpenFileDialog.ShowDialog(Me) =
    System.Windows.Forms.DialogResult.OK) Then
    Dim FileName As String = OpenFileDialog.FileName
    Dim pos As Integer = InStrRev(FileName, "\")
    TextBox1.Text = Mid(FileName, 1, pos - 1)
    TextBox2.Text = Mid(FileName, pos + 1, Len(FileName))
    Button3.Enabled = True
    End If

    End Sub

    Private Sub Form1_Load(sender As System.Object, e As
    System.EventArgs) Handles MyBase.Load

    End Sub
```

```
End Class
```

And here's what the form looks like:

View and Generate Event Log messages

When you are working with Management Packs, being able to see them work or not work in the way you wrote them is an important part of functionality testing.

The problem is you not only need to be able to see the event log messages show up, you also need to create them.

```
Imports System.Diagnostics
Public Class Form1

Dim EType As Integer

Private Sub Form1_Load(sender As System.Object, e As
System.EventArgs) Handles MyBase.Load

Dim ets() As EventLog = EventLog.GetEventLogs()
For Each et As EventLog In ets
ComboBox1.Items.Add(et.LogDisplayName)
ComboBox4.Items.Add(et.LogDisplayName)
Next


End Sub

Private Sub Button2_Click(sender As System.Object, e As
System.EventArgs)
```

```vb
End Sub

Private Sub ComboBox1_SelectedIndexChanged(sender As
System.Object, e As System.EventArgs) Handles
ComboBox1.SelectedIndexChanged


ComboBox2.Items.Clear()

Dim odic1 As Object = CreateObject("Scripting.Dictionary")
Dim ets() As EventLog = EventLog.GetEventLogs()
For Each evt As EventLog In ets
If evt.LogDisplayName = ComboBox1.Text Then
For Each ent As EventLogEntry In evt.Entries
If odic1.Exists(ent.Source) = False Then
ComboBox2.Items.Add(ent.Source)
odic1.Add(ent.Source, ent.Source)
End If
Next
End If
Next


End Sub

Private Sub ComboBox2_SelectedIndexChanged(sender As
System.Object, e As System.EventArgs) Handles
ComboBox2.SelectedIndexChanged

If ComboBox2.Text = "*Select A Source*" Then Exit Sub


DataGridView1.Rows.Clear()

Dim y As Integer = 0
Dim objs As Object =
GetObject("winmgmts:\\.\root\cimv2").ExecQuery("Select EventType,
EventIdentifier, SourceName, Message from Win32_NTLogEvent where
logFile='" & ComboBox1.Text & "' And SourceName = '" &
ComboBox2.Text & "'")
For Each obj In objs
Application.DoEvents()
DataGridView1.Rows.Add()
DataGridView1.Rows(y).Cells(0).Value = GetValue("EventType", obj)
```

```vbnet
DataGridView1.Rows(y).Cells(1).Value =
GetValue("EventIdentifier", obj)
DataGridView1.Rows(y).Cells(2).Value = GetValue("TimeWritten",
obj)
DataGridView1.Rows(y).Cells(3).Value = GetValue("SourceName",
obj)
DataGridView1.Rows(y).Cells(4).Value = GetValue("Message", obj)
y = y + 1
Next


End Sub
Private Function GetValue(ByVal Name As String, ByVal mo As
Object) As String

Dim pos As Integer
Dim tempstr As String


pos = InStr(mo.GetObjectText_, Name & " = ")

If pos = 0 Then
Return ""
End If


tempstr = Mid(mo.GetObjectText_, pos + Len(Name & " = "),
Len(mo.GetObjectText_))

pos = InStr(tempstr, ";")

tempstr = Mid(tempstr, 1, pos - 1)
tempstr = Replace(tempstr, Chr(34), "")
tempstr = Replace(tempstr, "{", "")
tempstr = Replace(tempstr, "}", "")
tempstr = Trim(tempstr)


If (mo.Properties_.Item(Name).CIMType = 101) And Len(tempstr) >
13 Then
Return tempstr.Substring(4, 2) & "/" & _
tempstr.Substring(6, 2) & "/" & _
tempstr.Substring(0, 4) & " " & _
tempstr.Substring(8, 2) & ":" & _
tempstr.Substring(10, 2) & ":" & _
```

```
tempstr.Substring(12, 2)
Exit Function
Else

Return tempstr

End If

End Function

Private Sub DataGridView1_MouseUp(ByVal sender As Object, ByVal e
As MouseEventArgs) Handles DataGridView1.MouseUp


Dim fso As Object = CreateObject("Scripting.FileSystemObject")
Dim txtstream As Object =
fso.OpenTextFile(System.Environment.CurrentDirectory & "\" &
ComboBox1.Text & ".html", 2, True, -2)
txtstream.WriteLine("<hmtl>")
txtstream.WriteLine("<head>")
txtstream.WriteLine("<title></title>")
txtstream.WriteLine("<style type='text/css'>")
txtstream.WriteLine("th")
txtstream.WriteLine("{")
txtstream.WriteLine("     COLOR: darkred;")
txtstream.WriteLine("     BACKGROUND-COLOR: #eeeeee;")
txtstream.WriteLine("          FONT-FAMILY:font-family:  Cambria,
serif;")
txtstream.WriteLine("     FONT-SIZE: 12px;")
txtstream.WriteLine("     text-align: left;")
txtstream.WriteLine("     white-Space: nowrap;")
txtstream.WriteLine("}")
txtstream.WriteLine("td")
txtstream.WriteLine("{")
txtstream.WriteLine("     COLOR: navy;")
txtstream.WriteLine("     BACKGROUND-COLOR: #eeeeee;")
txtstream.WriteLine("          FONT-FAMILY:  font-family:  Cambria,
serif;")
txtstream.WriteLine("     FONT-SIZE: 12px;")
txtstream.WriteLine("     text-align: left;")
txtstream.WriteLine("     white-Space: nowrap;")
txtstream.WriteLine("}")
```

```vb
txtstream.WriteLine("</style>")
txtstream.WriteLine("</head>")
txtstream.WriteLine("<body>")
txtstream.writeline("<center>")
txtstream.writeline("<table Style=""Border:0;"">")
txtstream.writeline("<tr><TH Nowrap STYLE=""background-
color:white;FONT-WEIGHT:normal; FONT-SIZE: 48px; COLOR: navy;
FONT-STYLE: normal; FONT-FAMILY: Edwardian Script ITC"">Planet
MPs  </TH></tr>")
txtstream.writeline("</table>")
txtstream.writeline("<table style=border:Double;border-
width:1px;border-color:navy;cellpadding=2 cellspacing=2
Width=0>")
txtstream.writeline("<tr>")


Try
Dim objs As Object =
GetObject("winmgmts:\\.\root\cimv2").ExecQuery("Select * From
Win32_NTLogEvent where TimeWritten like '" &
DataGridView1.CurrentRow.Cells(1).Value & "' and EventIdentifier
='" & Trim(DataGridView1.CurrentRow.Cells(2).Value) & "'")
Dim obj = objs.ItemIndex(0)
For Each prop As Object In obj.Properties_
txtstream.writeline("    <tr><th align=""left"">" & prop.Name &
"</th><td>" & GetValue(prop.Name, obj) & "</td><tr>")
Next
Catch ex As Exception
Dim objs As Object =
GetObject("winmgmts:\\.\root\cimv2").ExecQuery("Select * From
Win32_NTLogEvent where TimeWritten like '" &
DataGridView1.CurrentRow.Cells(1).Value & "'")
For Each obj In objs
For Each prop As Object In obj.Properties_
txtstream.writeline("    <tr><th align=""left"">" & prop.Name &
"</th><td>" & GetValue(prop.Name, obj) & "</td><tr>")
Next
Next
End Try


txtstream.writeline("</table>")
txtstream.writeline("</body>")
txtstream.writeline("</html>")
txtstream.Close()
```

```vbnet
WebBrowser1.Navigate(System.Environment.CurrentDirectory & "\" &
ComboBox1.Text & ".html")

End Sub

Private Sub ComboBox3_SelectedIndexChanged(sender As
System.Object, e As System.EventArgs) Handles
ComboBox3.SelectedIndexChanged
Select Case ComboBox3.Text

Case "Error"

EType = 1


Case "Warning"

EType = 2

Case "Information"

EType = 3

Case "Security Audit Success"

EType = 4

Case "Security Audit Failure"

EType = 5

End Select
End Sub

Private Sub Button1_Click(sender As System.Object, e As
System.EventArgs) Handles Button1.Click


Select Case ComboBox3.Text

Case "Error"

EType = 1
```

```
Case "Warning"

EType = 2

Case "Information"

EType = 3

Case "Security Audit Success"

EType = 4

Case "Security Audit Failure"

EType = 5

End Select



DataGridView1.Rows.Clear()

Dim y As Integer = 0
Dim objs As Object =
GetObject("winmgmts:\\.\root\cimv2").ExecQuery("Select EventType,
TimeWritten, EventIdentifier, SourceName, Message from
Win32_NTLogEvent where logFile='" & ComboBox1.Text & "' And
EventType = '" & EType & "'")
For Each obj In objs
Application.DoEvents()
DataGridView1.Rows.Add()
Try
DataGridView1.Rows(y).Cells(0).Value = GetValue("EventType", obj)
DataGridView1.Rows(y).Cells(1).Value = GetValue("TimeWritten",
obj)
DataGridView1.Rows(y).Cells(2).Value =
GetValue("EventIdentifier", obj)
DataGridView1.Rows(y).Cells(3).Value = GetValue("SourceName",
obj)
DataGridView1.Rows(y).Cells(4).Value = GetValue("Message", obj)
y = y + 1
Catch ex As Exception
```

```vbnet
End Try

Next

End Sub

Private Sub ComboBox4_SelectedIndexChanged(sender As
System.Object, e As System.EventArgs) Handles
ComboBox4.SelectedIndexChanged

If ComboBox4.Text <> "*Select An EventLog*" Then

ComboBox5.Items.Clear()

Dim odic1 As Object = CreateObject("Scripting.Dictionary")
Dim ets() As EventLog = EventLog.GetEventLogs()
For Each evt As EventLog In ets
If evt.LogDisplayName = ComboBox4.Text Then
For Each ent As EventLogEntry In evt.Entries
If odic1.Exists(ent.Source) = False Then
ComboBox5.Items.Add(ent.Source)
odic1.Add(ent.Source, ent.Source)
End If
Next
End If
Next

End If

End Sub

Private Sub ComboBox5_SelectedIndexChanged(sender As
System.Object, e As System.EventArgs) Handles
ComboBox5.SelectedIndexChanged

If ComboBox5.Text <> "*Select A Source*" Then
TextBox1.Text = ComboBox5.Text
Else
TextBox1.Text = ""
End If


End Sub
```

```vb
Private Sub Button2_Click_1(sender As System.Object, e As
System.EventArgs) Handles Button2.Click
If ComboBox4.Text = "*Select An EventLog*" Then
MsgBox("Please select an eventlog from the create event combobox
before clicking here.")
Exit Sub
End If

If TextBox1.Text = "" Then
MsgBox("Please either select a source from the create event
comobobox before click here.")
Exit Sub
End If

If TextBox1.Text <> ComboBox5.Text Then
Dim iret As Integer = MsgBox("Since the TextBox1.text isn't the
same as the text in the Combobox, do you want to register an
event source with the " & ComboBox4.Text & " EventLog?",
MsgBoxStyle.YesNo, "Register an event source")
If iret <> 6 Then
Exit Sub
End If
End If

If RichTextBox1.Text = "" Then
MsgBox("Please type in a message before clicking here.")
Exit Sub
End If


Dim evt As EventLog = Nothing
Dim ets() As EventLog = EventLog.GetEventLogs()
For Each evt In ets
If evt.LogDisplayName = ComboBox4.Text Then
Exit For
End If
Next

If evt.SourceExists(TextBox1.Text) = True Then

MsgBox("A source by that name already exists.")

Else

evt.CreateEventSource(TextBox1.Text, evt.LogDisplayName)
```

```vbnet
End If

Dim elt As New EventLog(ComboBox4.Text,
System.Environment.MachineName, TextBox1.Text)

Select Case ComboBox6.Text

Case "Error"

elt.WriteEntry(RichTextBox1.Text, EventLogEntryType.Error)

Case "Warning"

elt.WriteEntry(RichTextBox1.Text, EventLogEntryType.Warning)

Case "Information"

elt.WriteEntry(RichTextBox1.Text, EventLogEntryType.Information)

Case "Security Audit Success"

elt.WriteEntry(RichTextBox1.Text, EventLogEntryType.SuccessAudit)

Case "Security Audit Failure"

elt.WriteEntry(RichTextBox1.Text, EventLogEntryType.FailureAudit)

End Select

End Sub

End Class
```

And here's the view:

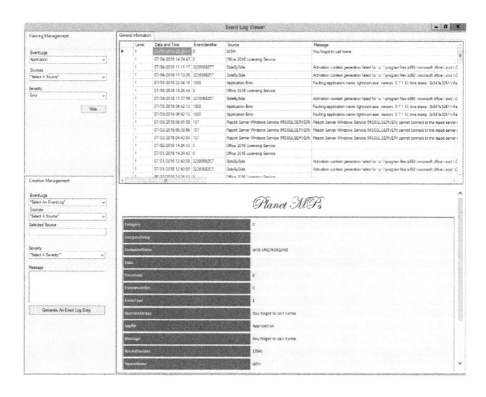

Stylesheets

Decorating your web pages

BELOW ARE SOME STYLESHEETS I COOKED UP THAT I LIKE AND THINK YOU MIGHT TOO. Don't worry I won't be offended if you take and modify to your hearts delight. Please do!

Here is one example of using the shadow box with a textbox:

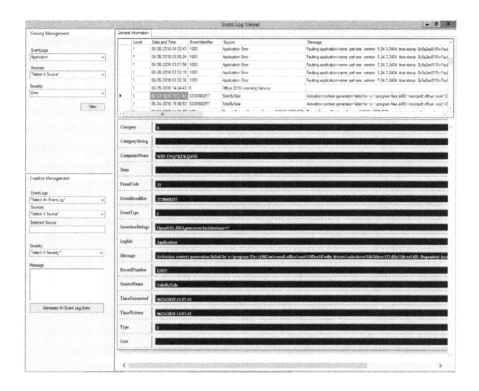

```
txtstream.WriteLine("<style type='text/css'>")

txtstream.WriteLine("th")

txtstream.WriteLine("{")

txtstream.WriteLine("    COLOR: white;")

txtstream.WriteLine("}")

txtstream.WriteLine("td")

txtstream.WriteLine("{")

txtstream.WriteLine("    COLOR: white;")

txtstream.WriteLine("}")
```

```
txtstream.WriteLine("</style>")
```

BLACK AND WHITE TEXT

```
txtstream.WriteLine("<style type='text/css'>")

txtstream.WriteLine("th")

txtstream.WriteLine("{")

txtstream.WriteLine("   COLOR: white;")

txtstream.WriteLine("   BACKGROUND-COLOR: black;")

txtstream.WriteLine("   FONT-FAMILY:font-family: Cambria, serif;")

txtstream.WriteLine("   FONT-SIZE: 12px;")

txtstream.WriteLine("   text-align: left;")

txtstream.WriteLine("   white-Space: nowrap;")

txtstream.WriteLine("}")

txtstream.WriteLine("td")

txtstream.WriteLine("{")

txtstream.WriteLine("   COLOR: white;")

txtstream.WriteLine("   BACKGROUND-COLOR: black;")

txtstream.WriteLine("   FONT-FAMILY: font-family: Cambria, serif;")

txtstream.WriteLine("   FONT-SIZE: 12px;")

txtstream.WriteLine("   text-align: left;")

txtstream.WriteLine("   white-Space: nowrap;")

txtstream.WriteLine("}")

txtstream.WriteLine("div")
```

```
txtstream.WriteLine("{")
txtstream.WriteLine("    COLOR: white;")
txtstream.WriteLine("    BACKGROUND-COLOR: black;")
txtstream.WriteLine("    FONT-FAMILY: font-family: Cambria, serif;")
txtstream.WriteLine("    FONT-SIZE: 10px;")
txtstream.WriteLine("    text-align: left;")
txtstream.WriteLine("    white-Space: nowrap;")
txtstream.WriteLine("}")
txtstream.WriteLine("span")
txtstream.WriteLine("{")
txtstream.WriteLine("    COLOR: white;")
txtstream.WriteLine("    BACKGROUND-COLOR: black;")
txtstream.WriteLine("    FONT-FAMILY: font-family: Cambria, serif;")
txtstream.WriteLine("    FONT-SIZE: 10px;")
txtstream.WriteLine("    text-align: left;")
txtstream.WriteLine("    white-Space: nowrap;")
txtstream.WriteLine("    display:inline-block;")
txtstream.WriteLine("    width: 100%;")
txtstream.WriteLine("}")
txtstream.WriteLine("textarea")
txtstream.WriteLine("{")
txtstream.WriteLine("    COLOR: white;")
txtstream.WriteLine("    BACKGROUND-COLOR: black;")
txtstream.WriteLine("    FONT-FAMILY: font-family: Cambria, serif;")
```

```
txtstream.WriteLine("    FONT-SIZE: 10px;")

txtstream.WriteLine("    text-align: left;")

txtstream.WriteLine("    white-Space: nowrap;")

txtstream.WriteLine("    width: 100%;")

txtstream.WriteLine("}")

txtstream.WriteLine("select")

txtstream.WriteLine("{")

txtstream.WriteLine("    COLOR: white;")

txtstream.WriteLine("    BACKGROUND-COLOR: black;")

txtstream.WriteLine("    FONT-FAMILY: font-family: Cambria, serif;")

txtstream.WriteLine("    FONT-SIZE: 10px;")

txtstream.WriteLine("    text-align: left;")

txtstream.WriteLine("    white-Space: nowrap;")

txtstream.WriteLine("    width: 100%;")

txtstream.WriteLine("}")

txtstream.WriteLine("input")

txtstream.WriteLine("{")

txtstream.WriteLine("    COLOR: white;")

txtstream.WriteLine("    BACKGROUND-COLOR: black;")

txtstream.WriteLine("    FONT-FAMILY: font-family: Cambria, serif;")

txtstream.WriteLine("    FONT-SIZE: 12px;")

txtstream.WriteLine("    text-align: left;")

txtstream.WriteLine("    display:table-cell;")

txtstream.WriteLine("    white-Space: nowrap;")
```

```
txtstream.WriteLine("}")

txtstream.WriteLine("h1 {")

txtstream.WriteLine("color: antiquewhite;")

txtstream.WriteLine("text-shadow: 1px 1px 1px black;")

txtstream.WriteLine("padding: 3px;")

txtstream.WriteLine("text-align: center;")

txtstream.WriteLine("box-shadow: inset 2px 2px 5px rgba(0,0,0,0.5), inset -2px -2px 5px rgba(255,255,255,0.5);")

txtstream.WriteLine("}")

txtstream.WriteLine("</style>")
```

COLORED TEXT

```
txtstream.WriteLine("<style type='text/css'>")

txtstream.WriteLine("th")

txtstream.WriteLine("{")

txtstream.WriteLine("    COLOR: darkred;")

txtstream.WriteLine("    BACKGROUND-COLOR: #eeeeee;")

txtstream.WriteLine("    FONT-FAMILY:font-family: Cambria, serif;")

txtstream.WriteLine("    FONT-SIZE: 12px;")

txtstream.WriteLine("    text-align: left;")

txtstream.WriteLine("    white-Space: nowrap;")

txtstream.WriteLine("}")

txtstream.WriteLine("td")
```

```
txtstream.WriteLine("{")

txtstream.WriteLine("   COLOR: navy;")

txtstream.WriteLine("   BACKGROUND-COLOR: #eeeeee;")

txtstream.WriteLine("   FONT-FAMILY: font-family: Cambria, serif;")

txtstream.WriteLine("   FONT-SIZE: 12px;")

txtstream.WriteLine("   text-align: left;")

txtstream.WriteLine("   white-Space: nowrap;")

txtstream.WriteLine("}")

txtstream.WriteLine("div")

txtstream.WriteLine("{")

txtstream.WriteLine("   COLOR: white;")

txtstream.WriteLine("   BACKGROUND-COLOR: navy;")

txtstream.WriteLine("   FONT-FAMILY: font-family: Cambria, serif;")

txtstream.WriteLine("   FONT-SIZE: 10px;")

txtstream.WriteLine("   text-align: left;")

txtstream.WriteLine("   white-Space: nowrap;")

txtstream.WriteLine("}")

txtstream.WriteLine("span")

txtstream.WriteLine("{")

txtstream.WriteLine("   COLOR: white;")

txtstream.WriteLine("   BACKGROUND-COLOR: navy;")

txtstream.WriteLine("   FONT-FAMILY: font-family: Cambria, serif;")

txtstream.WriteLine("   FONT-SIZE: 10px;")

txtstream.WriteLine("   text-align: left;")
```

```
txtstream.WriteLine("    white-Space: nowrap;")

txtstream.WriteLine("    display:inline-block;")

txtstream.WriteLine("    width: 100%;")

txtstream.WriteLine("}")

txtstream.WriteLine("textarea")

txtstream.WriteLine("{")

txtstream.WriteLine("    COLOR: white;")

txtstream.WriteLine("    BACKGROUND-COLOR: navy;")

txtstream.WriteLine("    FONT-FAMILY: font-family: Cambria, serif;")

txtstream.WriteLine("    FONT-SIZE: 10px;")

txtstream.WriteLine("    text-align: left;")

txtstream.WriteLine("    white-Space: nowrap;")

txtstream.WriteLine("    width: 100%;")

txtstream.WriteLine("}")

txtstream.WriteLine("select")

txtstream.WriteLine("{")

txtstream.WriteLine("    COLOR: white;")

txtstream.WriteLine("    BACKGROUND-COLOR: navy;")

txtstream.WriteLine("    FONT-FAMILY: font-family: Cambria, serif;")

txtstream.WriteLine("    FONT-SIZE: 10px;")

txtstream.WriteLine("    text-align: left;")

txtstream.WriteLine("    white-Space: nowrap;")

txtstream.WriteLine("    width: 100%;")

txtstream.WriteLine("}")
```

```
txtstream.WriteLine("input")

txtstream.WriteLine("{")

txtstream.WriteLine("    COLOR: white;")

txtstream.WriteLine("    BACKGROUND-COLOR: navy;")

txtstream.WriteLine("    FONT-FAMILY: font-family: Cambria, serif;")

txtstream.WriteLine("    FONT-SIZE: 12px;")

txtstream.WriteLine("    text-align: left;")

txtstream.WriteLine("    display:table-cell;")

txtstream.WriteLine("    white-Space: nowrap;")

txtstream.WriteLine("}")

txtstream.WriteLine("h1 {")

txtstream.WriteLine("color: antiquewhite;")

txtstream.WriteLine("text-shadow: 1px 1px 1px black;")

txtstream.WriteLine("padding: 3px;")

txtstream.WriteLine("text-align: center;")

txtstream.WriteLine("box-shadow: inset 2px 2px 5px rgba(0,0,0,0.5), inset -2px -2px 5px rgba(255,255,255,0.5);")

txtstream.WriteLine("}")

txtstream.WriteLine("</style>")
```

OSCILLATING ROW COLORS

```
txtstream.WriteLine("<style>")

txtstream.WriteLine("th")

txtstream.WriteLine("{")

txtstream.WriteLine("    COLOR: white;")

txtstream.WriteLine("    BACKGROUND-COLOR: navy;")

txtstream.WriteLine("    FONT-FAMILY:font-family: Cambria, serif;")

txtstream.WriteLine("    FONT-SIZE: 12px;")

txtstream.WriteLine("    text-align: left;")

txtstream.WriteLine("    white-Space: nowrap;")

txtstream.WriteLine("}")

txtstream.WriteLine("td")

txtstream.WriteLine("{")

txtstream.WriteLine("    COLOR: navy;")

txtstream.WriteLine("    FONT-FAMILY: font-family: Cambria, serif;")

txtstream.WriteLine("    FONT-SIZE: 12px;")

txtstream.WriteLine("    text-align: left;")

txtstream.WriteLine("    white-Space: nowrap;")

txtstream.WriteLine("}")

txtstream.WriteLine("div")

txtstream.WriteLine("{")

txtstream.WriteLine("    COLOR: navy;")

txtstream.WriteLine("    FONT-FAMILY: font-family: Cambria, serif;")

txtstream.WriteLine("    FONT-SIZE: 12px;")

txtstream.WriteLine("    text-align: left;")
```

```
txtstream.WriteLine("   white-Space: nowrap;")

txtstream.WriteLine("}")

txtstream.WriteLine("span")

txtstream.WriteLine("{")

txtstream.WriteLine("   COLOR: navy;")

txtstream.WriteLine("   FONT-FAMILY: font-family: Cambria, serif;")

txtstream.WriteLine("   FONT-SIZE: 12px;")

txtstream.WriteLine("   text-align: left;")

txtstream.WriteLine("   white-Space: nowrap;")

txtstream.WriteLine("   width: 100%;")

txtstream.WriteLine("}")

txtstream.WriteLine("textarea")

txtstream.WriteLine("{")

txtstream.WriteLine("   COLOR: navy;")

txtstream.WriteLine("   FONT-FAMILY: font-family: Cambria, serif;")

txtstream.WriteLine("   FONT-SIZE: 12px;")

txtstream.WriteLine("   text-align: left;")

txtstream.WriteLine("   white-Space: nowrap;")

txtstream.WriteLine("   display:inline-block;")

txtstream.WriteLine("   width: 100%;")

txtstream.WriteLine("}")

txtstream.WriteLine("select")

txtstream.WriteLine("{")

txtstream.WriteLine("   COLOR: navy;")
```

```
txtstream.WriteLine("    FONT-FAMILY: font-family: Cambria, serif;")

txtstream.WriteLine("    FONT-SIZE: 10px;")

txtstream.WriteLine("    text-align: left;")

txtstream.WriteLine("    white-Space: nowrap;")

txtstream.WriteLine("    display:inline-block;")

txtstream.WriteLine("    width: 100%;")

txtstream.WriteLine("}")

txtstream.WriteLine("input")

txtstream.WriteLine("{")

txtstream.WriteLine("    COLOR: navy;")

txtstream.WriteLine("    FONT-FAMILY: font-family: Cambria, serif;")

txtstream.WriteLine("    FONT-SIZE: 12px;")

txtstream.WriteLine("    text-align: left;")

txtstream.WriteLine("    display:table-cell;")

txtstream.WriteLine("    white-Space: nowrap;")

txtstream.WriteLine("}")

txtstream.WriteLine("h1 {")

txtstream.WriteLine("color: antiquewhite;")

txtstream.WriteLine("text-shadow: 1px 1px 1px black;")

txtstream.WriteLine("padding: 3px;")

txtstream.WriteLine("text-align: center;")

txtstream.WriteLine("box-shadow: inset 2px 2px 5px rgba(0,0,0,0.5), inset -2px -2px 5px rgba(255,255,255,0.5);")

txtstream.WriteLine("}")
```

```
txtstream.WriteLine("tr:nth-child(even){background-color:#f2f2f2;}")
txtstream.WriteLine("tr:nth-child(odd){background-color:#cccccc; color:#f2f2f2;}")
txtstream.WriteLine("</style>")
```

GHOST DECORATED

```
txtstream.WriteLine("<style type='text/css'>")
txtstream.WriteLine("th")
txtstream.WriteLine("{")
txtstream.WriteLine("   COLOR: black;")
txtstream.WriteLine("   BACKGROUND-COLOR: white;")
txtstream.WriteLine("   FONT-FAMILY:font-family: Cambria, serif;")
txtstream.WriteLine("   FONT-SIZE: 12px;")
txtstream.WriteLine("   text-align: left;")
txtstream.WriteLine("   white-Space: nowrap;")
txtstream.WriteLine("}")
txtstream.WriteLine("td")
txtstream.WriteLine("{")
txtstream.WriteLine("   COLOR: black;")
txtstream.WriteLine("   BACKGROUND-COLOR: white;")
txtstream.WriteLine("   FONT-FAMILY: font-family: Cambria, serif;")
txtstream.WriteLine("   FONT-SIZE: 12px;")
txtstream.WriteLine("   text-align: left;")
txtstream.WriteLine("   white-Space: nowrap;")
```

```
txtstream.WriteLine("}")

txtstream.WriteLine("div")

txtstream.WriteLine("{")

txtstream.WriteLine("    COLOR: black;")

txtstream.WriteLine("    BACKGROUND-COLOR: white;")

txtstream.WriteLine("    FONT-FAMILY: font-family: Cambria, serif;")

txtstream.WriteLine("    FONT-SIZE: 10px;")

txtstream.WriteLine("    text-align: left;")

txtstream.WriteLine("    white-Space: nowrap;")

txtstream.WriteLine("}")

txtstream.WriteLine("span")

txtstream.WriteLine("{")

txtstream.WriteLine("    COLOR: black;")

txtstream.WriteLine("    BACKGROUND-COLOR: white;")

txtstream.WriteLine("    FONT-FAMILY: font-family: Cambria, serif;")

txtstream.WriteLine("    FONT-SIZE: 10px;")

txtstream.WriteLine("    text-align: left;")

txtstream.WriteLine("    white-Space: nowrap;")

txtstream.WriteLine("    display:inline-block;")

txtstream.WriteLine("    width: 100%;")

txtstream.WriteLine("}")

txtstream.WriteLine("textarea")

txtstream.WriteLine("{")

txtstream.WriteLine("    COLOR: black;")
```

```
txtstream.WriteLine("   BACKGROUND-COLOR: white;")

txtstream.WriteLine("   FONT-FAMILY: font-family: Cambria, serif;")

txtstream.WriteLine("   FONT-SIZE: 10px;")

txtstream.WriteLine("   text-align: left;")

txtstream.WriteLine("   white-Space: nowrap;")

txtstream.WriteLine("   width: 100%;")

txtstream.WriteLine("}")

txtstream.WriteLine("select")

txtstream.WriteLine("{")

txtstream.WriteLine("   COLOR: black;")

txtstream.WriteLine("   BACKGROUND-COLOR: white;")

txtstream.WriteLine("   FONT-FAMILY: font-family: Cambria, serif;")

txtstream.WriteLine("   FONT-SIZE: 10px;")

txtstream.WriteLine("   text-align: left;")

txtstream.WriteLine("   white-Space: nowrap;")

txtstream.WriteLine("   width: 100%;")

txtstream.WriteLine("}")

txtstream.WriteLine("input")

txtstream.WriteLine("{")

txtstream.WriteLine("   COLOR: black;")

txtstream.WriteLine("   BACKGROUND-COLOR: white;")

txtstream.WriteLine("   FONT-FAMILY: font-family: Cambria, serif;")

txtstream.WriteLine("   FONT-SIZE: 12px;")

txtstream.WriteLine("   text-align: left;")
```

```
txtstream.WriteLine("    display:table-cell;")

txtstream.WriteLine("    white-Space: nowrap;")

txtstream.WriteLine("}")

txtstream.WriteLine("h1 {")

txtstream.WriteLine("color: antiquewhite;")

txtstream.WriteLine("text-shadow: 1px 1px 1px black;")

txtstream.WriteLine("padding: 3px;")

txtstream.WriteLine("text-align: center;")

txtstream.WriteLine("box-shadow: inset 2px 2px 5px rgba(0,0,0,0.5), inset -2px -2px 5px rgba(255,255,255,0.5);")

txtstream.WriteLine("}")

txtstream.WriteLine("</style>")
```

3D

```
txtstream.WriteLine("<style type='text/css'>")

txtstream.WriteLine("body")

txtstream.WriteLine("{")

txtstream.WriteLine("    PADDING-RIGHT: 0px;")

txtstream.WriteLine("    PADDING-LEFT: 0px;")

txtstream.WriteLine("    PADDING-BOTTOM: 0px;")

txtstream.WriteLine("    MARGIN: 0px;")

txtstream.WriteLine("    COLOR: #333;")
```

```
txtstream.WriteLine("    PADDING-TOP: 0px;")

txtstream.WriteLine("    FONT-FAMILY: verdana, arial, helvetica, sans-serif;")

txtstream.WriteLine("}")

txtstream.WriteLine("table")

txtstream.WriteLine("{")

txtstream.WriteLine("    BORDER-RIGHT: #999999 3px solid;")

txtstream.WriteLine("    PADDING-RIGHT: 6px;")

txtstream.WriteLine("    PADDING-LEFT: 6px;")

txtstream.WriteLine("    FONT-WEIGHT: Bold;")

txtstream.WriteLine("    FONT-SIZE: 14px;")

txtstream.WriteLine("    PADDING-BOTTOM: 6px;")

txtstream.WriteLine("    COLOR: Peru;")

txtstream.WriteLine("    LINE-HEIGHT: 14px;")

txtstream.WriteLine("    PADDING-TOP: 6px;")

txtstream.WriteLine("    BORDER-BOTTOM: #999 1px solid;")

txtstream.WriteLine("    BACKGROUND-COLOR: #eeeeee;")

txtstream.WriteLine("    FONT-FAMILY: verdana, arial, helvetica, sans-serif;")

txtstream.WriteLine("    FONT-SIZE: 12px;")

txtstream.WriteLine("}")

txtstream.WriteLine("th")

txtstream.WriteLine("{")

txtstream.WriteLine("    BORDER-RIGHT: #999999 3px solid;")

txtstream.WriteLine("    PADDING-RIGHT: 6px;")

txtstream.WriteLine("    PADDING-LEFT: 6px;")
```

```
txtstream.WriteLine("    FONT-WEIGHT: Bold;")

txtstream.WriteLine("    FONT-SIZE: 14px;")

txtstream.WriteLine("    PADDING-BOTTOM: 6px;")

txtstream.WriteLine("    COLOR: darkred;")

txtstream.WriteLine("    LINE-HEIGHT: 14px;")

txtstream.WriteLine("    PADDING-TOP: 6px;")

txtstream.WriteLine("    BORDER-BOTTOM: #999 1px solid;")

txtstream.WriteLine("    BACKGROUND-COLOR: #eeeeee;")

txtstream.WriteLine("    FONT-FAMILY:font-family: Cambria, serif;")

txtstream.WriteLine("    FONT-SIZE: 12px;")

txtstream.WriteLine("    text-align: left;")

txtstream.WriteLine("    white-Space: nowrap;")

txtstream.WriteLine("}")

txtstream.WriteLine(".th")

txtstream.WriteLine("{")

txtstream.WriteLine("    BORDER-RIGHT: #999999 2px solid;")

txtstream.WriteLine("    PADDING-RIGHT: 6px;")

txtstream.WriteLine("    PADDING-LEFT: 6px;")

txtstream.WriteLine("    FONT-WEIGHT: Bold;")

txtstream.WriteLine("    PADDING-BOTTOM: 6px;")

txtstream.WriteLine("    COLOR: black;")

txtstream.WriteLine("    PADDING-TOP: 6px;")

txtstream.WriteLine("    BORDER-BOTTOM: #999 2px solid;")

txtstream.WriteLine("    BACKGROUND-COLOR: #eeeeee;")
```

```
txtstream.WriteLine("    FONT-FAMILY: font-family: Cambria, serif;")

txtstream.WriteLine("    FONT-SIZE: 10px;")

txtstream.WriteLine("    text-align: right;")

txtstream.WriteLine("    white-Space: nowrap;")

txtstream.WriteLine("}")

txtstream.WriteLine("td")

txtstream.WriteLine("{")

txtstream.WriteLine("    BORDER-RIGHT: #999999 3px solid;")

txtstream.WriteLine("    PADDING-RIGHT: 6px;")

txtstream.WriteLine("    PADDING-LEFT: 6px;")

txtstream.WriteLine("    FONT-WEIGHT: Normal;")

txtstream.WriteLine("    PADDING-BOTTOM: 6px;")

txtstream.WriteLine("    COLOR: navy;")

txtstream.WriteLine("    LINE-HEIGHT: 14px;")

txtstream.WriteLine("    PADDING-TOP: 6px;")

txtstream.WriteLine("    BORDER-BOTTOM: #999 1px solid;")

txtstream.WriteLine("    BACKGROUND-COLOR: #eeeeee;")

txtstream.WriteLine("    FONT-FAMILY: font-family: Cambria, serif;")

txtstream.WriteLine("    FONT-SIZE: 12px;")

txtstream.WriteLine("    text-align: left;")

txtstream.WriteLine("    white-Space: nowrap;")

txtstream.WriteLine("}")

txtstream.WriteLine("div")

txtstream.WriteLine("{")
```

```
txtstream.WriteLine("    BORDER-RIGHT: #999999 3px solid;")

txtstream.WriteLine("    PADDING-RIGHT: 6px;")

txtstream.WriteLine("    PADDING-LEFT: 6px;")

txtstream.WriteLine("    FONT-WEIGHT: Normal;")

txtstream.WriteLine("    PADDING-BOTTOM: 6px;")

txtstream.WriteLine("    COLOR: white;")

txtstream.WriteLine("    PADDING-TOP: 6px;")

txtstream.WriteLine("    BORDER-BOTTOM: #999 1px solid;")

txtstream.WriteLine("    BACKGROUND-COLOR: navy;")

txtstream.WriteLine("    FONT-FAMILY: font-family: Cambria, serif;")

txtstream.WriteLine("    FONT-SIZE: 10px;")

txtstream.WriteLine("    text-align: left;")

txtstream.WriteLine("    white-Space: nowrap;")

txtstream.WriteLine("}")

txtstream.WriteLine("span")

txtstream.WriteLine("{")

txtstream.WriteLine("    BORDER-RIGHT: #999999 3px solid;")

txtstream.WriteLine("    PADDING-RIGHT: 3px;")

txtstream.WriteLine("    PADDING-LEFT: 3px;")

txtstream.WriteLine("    FONT-WEIGHT: Normal;")

txtstream.WriteLine("    PADDING-BOTTOM: 3px;")

txtstream.WriteLine("    COLOR: white;")

txtstream.WriteLine("    PADDING-TOP: 3px;")

txtstream.WriteLine("    BORDER-BOTTOM: #999 1px solid;")
```

```
txtstream.WriteLine("    BACKGROUND-COLOR: navy;")
txtstream.WriteLine("    FONT-FAMILY: font-family: Cambria, serif;")
txtstream.WriteLine("    FONT-SIZE: 10px;")
txtstream.WriteLine("    text-align: left;")
txtstream.WriteLine("    white-Space: nowrap;")
txtstream.WriteLine("    display:inline-block;")
txtstream.WriteLine("    width: 100%;")
txtstream.WriteLine("}")
txtstream.WriteLine("textarea")
txtstream.WriteLine("{")
txtstream.WriteLine("    BORDER-RIGHT: #999999 3px solid;")
txtstream.WriteLine("    PADDING-RIGHT: 3px;")
txtstream.WriteLine("    PADDING-LEFT: 3px;")
txtstream.WriteLine("    FONT-WEIGHT: Normal;")
txtstream.WriteLine("    PADDING-BOTTOM: 3px;")
txtstream.WriteLine("    COLOR: white;")
txtstream.WriteLine("    PADDING-TOP: 3px;")
txtstream.WriteLine("    BORDER-BOTTOM: #999 1px solid;")
txtstream.WriteLine("    BACKGROUND-COLOR: navy;")
txtstream.WriteLine("    FONT-FAMILY: font-family: Cambria, serif;")
txtstream.WriteLine("    FONT-SIZE: 10px;")
txtstream.WriteLine("    text-align: left;")
txtstream.WriteLine("    white-Space: nowrap;")
txtstream.WriteLine("    width: 100%;")
```

```
txtstream.WriteLine("}")

txtstream.WriteLine("select")

txtstream.WriteLine("{")

txtstream.WriteLine("    BORDER-RIGHT: #999999 3px solid;")

txtstream.WriteLine("    PADDING-RIGHT: 6px;")

txtstream.WriteLine("    PADDING-LEFT: 6px;")

txtstream.WriteLine("    FONT-WEIGHT: Normal;")

txtstream.WriteLine("    PADDING-BOTTOM: 6px;")

txtstream.WriteLine("    COLOR: white;")

txtstream.WriteLine("    PADDING-TOP: 6px;")

txtstream.WriteLine("    BORDER-BOTTOM: #999 1px solid;")

txtstream.WriteLine("    BACKGROUND-COLOR: navy;")

txtstream.WriteLine("    FONT-FAMILY: font-family: Cambria, serif;")

txtstream.WriteLine("    FONT-SIZE: 10px;")

txtstream.WriteLine("    text-align: left;")

txtstream.WriteLine("    white-Space: nowrap;")

txtstream.WriteLine("    width: 100%;")

txtstream.WriteLine("}")

txtstream.WriteLine("input")

txtstream.WriteLine("{")

txtstream.WriteLine("    BORDER-RIGHT: #999999 3px solid;")

txtstream.WriteLine("    PADDING-RIGHT: 3px;")

txtstream.WriteLine("    PADDING-LEFT: 3px;")

txtstream.WriteLine("    FONT-WEIGHT: Bold;")
```

```
txtstream.WriteLine("    PADDING-BOTTOM: 3px;")

txtstream.WriteLine("    COLOR: white;")

txtstream.WriteLine("    PADDING-TOP: 3px;")

txtstream.WriteLine("    BORDER-BOTTOM: #999 1px solid;")

txtstream.WriteLine("    BACKGROUND-COLOR: navy;")

txtstream.WriteLine("    FONT-FAMILY: font-family: Cambria, serif;")

txtstream.WriteLine("    FONT-SIZE: 12px;")

txtstream.WriteLine("    text-align: left;")

txtstream.WriteLine("    display:table-cell;")

txtstream.WriteLine("    white-Space: nowrap;")

txtstream.WriteLine("    width: 100%;")

txtstream.WriteLine("}")

txtstream.WriteLine("h1 {")

txtstream.WriteLine("color: antiquewhite;")

txtstream.WriteLine("text-shadow: 1px 1px 1px black;")

txtstream.WriteLine("padding: 3px;")

txtstream.WriteLine("text-align: center;")

txtstream.WriteLine("box-shadow: inset 2px 2px 5px rgba(0,0,0,0.5), inset -2px -2px 5px rgba(255,255,255,0.5);")

txtstream.WriteLine("}")

txtstream.WriteLine("</style>")
```

SHADOW BOX

```
txtstream.WriteLine("<style type='text/css'>")

txtstream.WriteLine("body")

txtstream.WriteLine("{")

txtstream.WriteLine("   PADDING-RIGHT: 0px;")

txtstream.WriteLine("   PADDING-LEFT: 0px;")

txtstream.WriteLine("   PADDING-BOTTOM: 0px;")

txtstream.WriteLine("   MARGIN: 0px;")

txtstream.WriteLine("   COLOR: #333;")

txtstream.WriteLine("   PADDING-TOP: 0px;")

txtstream.WriteLine("   FONT-FAMILY: verdana, arial, helvetica, sans-serif;")

txtstream.WriteLine("}")

txtstream.WriteLine("table")

txtstream.WriteLine("{")

txtstream.WriteLine("   BORDER-RIGHT: #999999 1px solid;")

txtstream.WriteLine("   PADDING-RIGHT: 1px;")

txtstream.WriteLine("   PADDING-LEFT: 1px;")

txtstream.WriteLine("   PADDING-BOTTOM: 1px;")

txtstream.WriteLine("   LINE-HEIGHT: 8px;")

txtstream.WriteLine("   PADDING-TOP: 1px;")

txtstream.WriteLine("   BORDER-BOTTOM: #999 1px solid;")

txtstream.WriteLine("   BACKGROUND-COLOR: #eeeeee;")

txtstream.WriteLine("   filter:progid:DXImageTransform.Microsoft.Shadow(color='silver', Direction=135, Strength=16)")

txtstream.WriteLine("}")
```

```
txtstream.WriteLine("th")

txtstream.WriteLine("{")

txtstream.WriteLine("    BORDER-RIGHT: #999999 3px solid;")

txtstream.WriteLine("    PADDING-RIGHT: 6px;")

txtstream.WriteLine("    PADDING-LEFT: 6px;")

txtstream.WriteLine("    FONT-WEIGHT: Bold;")

txtstream.WriteLine("    FONT-SIZE: 14px;")

txtstream.WriteLine("    PADDING-BOTTOM: 6px;")

txtstream.WriteLine("    COLOR: darkred;")

txtstream.WriteLine("    LINE-HEIGHT: 14px;")

txtstream.WriteLine("    PADDING-TOP: 6px;")

txtstream.WriteLine("    BORDER-BOTTOM: #999 1px solid;")

txtstream.WriteLine("    BACKGROUND-COLOR: #eeeeee;")

txtstream.WriteLine("    FONT-FAMILY: font-family: Cambria, serif;")

txtstream.WriteLine("    FONT-SIZE: 12px;")

txtstream.WriteLine("    text-align: left;")

txtstream.WriteLine("    white-Space: nowrap;")

txtstream.WriteLine("}")

txtstream.WriteLine(".th")

txtstream.WriteLine("{")

txtstream.WriteLine("    BORDER-RIGHT: #999999 2px solid;")

txtstream.WriteLine("    PADDING-RIGHT: 6px;")

txtstream.WriteLine("    PADDING-LEFT: 6px;")

txtstream.WriteLine("    FONT-WEIGHT: Bold;")
```

```
txtstream.WriteLine("    PADDING-BOTTOM: 6px;")
txtstream.WriteLine("    COLOR: black;")
txtstream.WriteLine("    PADDING-TOP: 6px;")
txtstream.WriteLine("    BORDER-BOTTOM: #999 2px solid;")
txtstream.WriteLine("    BACKGROUND-COLOR: #eeeeee;")
txtstream.WriteLine("    FONT-FAMILY: font-family: Cambria, serif;")
txtstream.WriteLine("    FONT-SIZE: 10px;")
txtstream.WriteLine("    text-align: right;")
txtstream.WriteLine("    white-Space: nowrap;")
txtstream.WriteLine("}")
txtstream.WriteLine("td")
txtstream.WriteLine("{")
txtstream.WriteLine("    BORDER-RIGHT: #999999 3px solid;")
txtstream.WriteLine("    PADDING-RIGHT: 6px;")
txtstream.WriteLine("    PADDING-LEFT: 6px;")
txtstream.WriteLine("    FONT-WEIGHT: Normal;")
txtstream.WriteLine("    PADDING-BOTTOM: 6px;")
txtstream.WriteLine("    COLOR: navy;")
txtstream.WriteLine("    LINE-HEIGHT: 14px;")
txtstream.WriteLine("    PADDING-TOP: 6px;")
txtstream.WriteLine("    BORDER-BOTTOM: #999 1px solid;")
txtstream.WriteLine("    BACKGROUND-COLOR: #eeeeee;")
txtstream.WriteLine("    FONT-FAMILY: font-family: Cambria, serif;")
txtstream.WriteLine("    FONT-SIZE: 12px;")
```

```
txtstream.WriteLine("    text-align: left;")

txtstream.WriteLine("    white-Space: nowrap;")

txtstream.WriteLine("}")

txtstream.WriteLine("div")

txtstream.WriteLine("{")

txtstream.WriteLine("    BORDER-RIGHT: #999999 3px solid;")

txtstream.WriteLine("    PADDING-RIGHT: 6px;")

txtstream.WriteLine("    PADDING-LEFT: 6px;")

txtstream.WriteLine("    FONT-WEIGHT: Normal;")

txtstream.WriteLine("    PADDING-BOTTOM: 6px;")

txtstream.WriteLine("    COLOR: white;")

txtstream.WriteLine("    PADDING-TOP: 6px;")

txtstream.WriteLine("    BORDER-BOTTOM: #999 1px solid;")

txtstream.WriteLine("    BACKGROUND-COLOR: navy;")

txtstream.WriteLine("    FONT-FAMILY: font-family: Cambria, serif;")

txtstream.WriteLine("    FONT-SIZE: 10px;")

txtstream.WriteLine("    text-align: left;")

txtstream.WriteLine("    white-Space: nowrap;")

txtstream.WriteLine("}")

txtstream.WriteLine("span")

txtstream.WriteLine("{")

txtstream.WriteLine("    BORDER-RIGHT: #999999 3px solid;")

txtstream.WriteLine("    PADDING-RIGHT: 3px;")

txtstream.WriteLine("    PADDING-LEFT: 3px;")
```

```
txtstream.WriteLine("    FONT-WEIGHT: Normal;")

txtstream.WriteLine("    PADDING-BOTTOM: 3px;")

txtstream.WriteLine("    COLOR: white;")

txtstream.WriteLine("    PADDING-TOP: 3px;")

txtstream.WriteLine("    BORDER-BOTTOM: #999 1px solid;")

txtstream.WriteLine("    BACKGROUND-COLOR: navy;")

txtstream.WriteLine("    FONT-FAMILY: font-family: Cambria, serif;")

txtstream.WriteLine("    FONT-SIZE: 10px;")

txtstream.WriteLine("    text-align: left;")

txtstream.WriteLine("    white-Space: nowrap;")

txtstream.WriteLine("    display: inline-block;")

txtstream.WriteLine("    width: 100%;")

txtstream.WriteLine("}")

txtstream.WriteLine("textarea")

txtstream.WriteLine("{")

txtstream.WriteLine("    BORDER-RIGHT: #999999 3px solid;")

txtstream.WriteLine("    PADDING-RIGHT: 3px;")

txtstream.WriteLine("    PADDING-LEFT: 3px;")

txtstream.WriteLine("    FONT-WEIGHT: Normal;")

txtstream.WriteLine("    PADDING-BOTTOM: 3px;")

txtstream.WriteLine("    COLOR: white;")

txtstream.WriteLine("    PADDING-TOP: 3px;")

txtstream.WriteLine("    BORDER-BOTTOM: #999 1px solid;")

txtstream.WriteLine("    BACKGROUND-COLOR: navy;")
```

```
txtstream.WriteLine("   FONT-FAMILY: font-family: Cambria, serif;")

txtstream.WriteLine("   FONT-SIZE: 10px;")

txtstream.WriteLine("   text-align: left;")

txtstream.WriteLine("   white-Space: nowrap;")

txtstream.WriteLine("   width: 100%;")

txtstream.WriteLine("}")

txtstream.WriteLine("select")

txtstream.WriteLine("{")

txtstream.WriteLine("   BORDER-RIGHT: #999999 3px solid;")

txtstream.WriteLine("   PADDING-RIGHT: 6px;")

txtstream.WriteLine("   PADDING-LEFT: 6px;")

txtstream.WriteLine("   FONT-WEIGHT: Normal;")

txtstream.WriteLine("   PADDING-BOTTOM: 6px;")

txtstream.WriteLine("   COLOR: white;")

txtstream.WriteLine("   PADDING-TOP: 6px;")

txtstream.WriteLine("   BORDER-BOTTOM: #999 1px solid;")

txtstream.WriteLine("   BACKGROUND-COLOR: navy;")

txtstream.WriteLine("   FONT-FAMILY: font-family: Cambria, serif;")

txtstream.WriteLine("   FONT-SIZE: 10px;")

txtstream.WriteLine("   text-align: left;")

txtstream.WriteLine("   white-Space: nowrap;")

txtstream.WriteLine("   width: 100%;")

txtstream.WriteLine("}")

txtstream.WriteLine("input")
```

```
txtstream.WriteLine("{")

txtstream.WriteLine("    BORDER-RIGHT: #999999 3px solid;")

txtstream.WriteLine("    PADDING-RIGHT: 3px;")

txtstream.WriteLine("    PADDING-LEFT: 3px;")

txtstream.WriteLine("    FONT-WEIGHT: Bold;")

txtstream.WriteLine("    PADDING-BOTTOM: 3px;")

txtstream.WriteLine("    COLOR: white;")

txtstream.WriteLine("    PADDING-TOP: 3px;")

txtstream.WriteLine("    BORDER-BOTTOM: #999 1px solid;")

txtstream.WriteLine("    BACKGROUND-COLOR: navy;")

txtstream.WriteLine("    FONT-FAMILY: font-family: Cambria, serif;")

txtstream.WriteLine("    FONT-SIZE: 12px;")

txtstream.WriteLine("    text-align: left;")

txtstream.WriteLine("    display: table-cell;")

txtstream.WriteLine("    white-Space: nowrap;")

txtstream.WriteLine("    width: 100%;")

txtstream.WriteLine("}")

txtstream.WriteLine("h1 {")

txtstream.WriteLine("color: antiquewhite;")

txtstream.WriteLine("text-shadow: 1px 1px 1px black;")

txtstream.WriteLine("padding: 3px;")

txtstream.WriteLine("text-align: center;")

txtstream.WriteLine("box-shadow: inset 2px 2px 5px rgba(0,0,0,0.5), inset -2px -2px 5px rgba(255,255,255,0.5);")
```

```
txtstream.WriteLine("}")

txtstream.WriteLine("</style>")
```

www.ingramcontent.com/pod-product-compliance
Lightning Source LLC
Chambersburg PA
CBHW070859070326
40690CB00009B/1916